ADOPT A SAILOR

Charles Evered

BROADWAY PLAY PUBLISHING INC
New York
www.broadwayplaypublishing.com
info@broadwayplaypublishing.com

ADOPT A SAILOR
© Copyright 2007 by Charles Evered

First printing: August 2007
Second printing: November 2013

I S B N: 978-0-88145-343-0

Book design: Marie Donovan
Typeface: Palatino
Printed and bound in the U S A

ADOPT A SAILOR first appeared as a ten minute play that ran from 9-11 September 2002, during the Brave New World event at Town Hall in New York City, commemorating the first anniversary of the terrorist attacks. The rotating cast for that production included: Bebe Neuwirth, Neil Patrick Harris, Amy Irving, Anne Jackson, Liev Schreiber, Eli Wallach, Sam Waterston and Michael Nouri. The directors included Erica Gould and Craig Carlisle.

ADOPT A SAILOR has been presented in several public readings and fundraising events. Actors that have graciously donated their services during those presentations have included: Len Cariou, Scott Cohen, Tom Costello, Wendy Rolfe Evered, Josh Fardon, Matthew Modine, Luke Perry, Amy Povich, Josh Radnor and Greg Spradlin. Directors have included: Morgan Murphy and Eric Barr.

ADOPT A SAILOR was first produced in a workshop production at The Payan Theatre in New York City, 29 March-1 April 2007. It was presented by U N Y Y C, (Unofficial New York Yale Cabaret). The cast and creative contributors were:

SAILOR . . . . Brian Slaten
RICHARD . . . . Maury Ginsberg
PATRICIA . . . . Sonya Rokes

Director . . . . Craig Carlisle
Costume design . . . . Karen Flood
Stage manager . . . . Brad Gore
Assistant director . . . . Ashley Kelly-Tata

Special thanks to the following board members of
U N Y Y C: Pun Bandhu, Josepth T Barna, Neal Lerner
and Heidi Seifert.

Very special thanks to Andy Breckman and Kip Gould.

CHARACTERS & SETTING

SAILOR, *early twenties*
RICHARD, *filmmaker*
PATRICIA, *gallery owner*

The play takes place in the dining/living area of RICHARD *and* PATRICIA'*s upscale apartment on the Upper West Side of New York City.*

The present, evening

FOR THREE GREAT MEN:

My father, Charles J Evered

Stan Kamin

and George Roy Hill

NOTES ON THE PLAY

ADOPT A SAILOR is a play meant to be easily
produced. My hope is that it will continue to be
produced in varied venues. Thus far, it has been
produced in traditional theaters, in living rooms and
in rehearsal halls. I would like it to expand into even
more varied spaces such as on military bases, in church
basements, V F W halls, American Legion posts,
backyards, college campuses, garages, classrooms,
outdoor theatres, high school stages, ships at sea, officer
and enlisted clubs, anywhere people might be open to
seeing or hearing it.

It's a play acting couples can easily perform. And it's
a play "non actors" can feel confident in reading or
appearing in as well.

If ADOPT A SAILOR is going to be presented as part
of a fundraiser, allow me to suggest two organizations
that are more than worthy of support:

Navy-Marine Corps Relief Society
875 North Randolf Street, Suite 225
Arlington, VA 22203-1977
Tel: 703-696-4904
www.nmcrs.org

Fisher House Foundation, Inc
1401 Rockville Pike, Suite 600
Rockville, MD 20852
Tel: 301-294-8560
www.fisherhouse.org

And finally, ADOPT A SAILOR is decidedly *not* a "liberal" or "conservative" play. It's a play about three human beings who normally wouldn't be in the same state let alone the same apartment together. Yet still, all three find they have more in common than they might have ever imagined. Simple as that.
Charles Evered
Princeton, New Jersey
April 15, 2007

(Prelude to Bach's Cello Suite Number One, then at rise: we see the SAILOR *standing inside the apartment. He seems to glow in his enlisted dress white uniform and has a green duffle bag slung over one shoulder.* RICHARD *stands across from him.)*

RICHARD: And she said *West* 76th Street. Not East. West 76th?

SAILOR: Yes, sir, in New York City.

RICHARD: Well, New York City is a big place.

SAILOR: Yes, sir.

RICHARD: You don't have to call me "sir."

SAILOR: No, sir. Maybe I should just go. I didn't mean to— *(He starts out.)*

RICHARD: —well, wait, wait, what else did the lady say? Who set up the appointment?

SAILOR: Appointment?

RICHARD: Yes, is there anything else on the piece of paper?

(The SAILOR *looks at the piece of paper.)*

SAILOR: There's a name on it.

RICHARD: And what is it?

SAILOR: "Patricia."

RICHARD: "Patricia" is my wife's name.

SAILOR: That's what it says, sir.

RICHARD: And what were you saying about an "adoption"?

SAILOR: Yes, sir. That's the name of the program: "Adopt a Sailor".

RICHARD: And so we're supposed to—what, we're supposed to "adopt" you?

SAILOR: Not in an actual, way. I believe it's meant more as a figure of speech.

RICHARD: I assumed as much.

SAILOR: Like I said, I didn't mean to—

RICHARD: —don't worry about it. My wife should be home any minute and we can get to the bottom of this. Come on in.

SAILOR: Are you sure?

RICHARD: Of course. I'm sure there's some kind of explanation. Put your bag down. Make yourself at home.

SAILOR: As long as I'm not—

RICHARD: —you're not, not at all.

(The SAILOR *leans his bag against the wall, slowly walks further in.* RICHARD *goes to a small bar, turns to him.*)

RICHARD: What's your pleasure?

SAILOR: Just a soda pop would be fine, thank you.

RICHARD: "A soda pop"? What kind of sailor are you?

SAILOR: Oh, I've never been much of a big drinker.

RICHARD: Okay, "soda pop" it is.

(RICHARD *hands him a glass of soda.* RICHARD *then pours himself a large glass of wine.*)

RICHARD: Sit!

(The SAILOR *sits.* RICHARD *sits across from him.)*

RICHARD: So, what are you?

SAILOR: Sir?

RICHARD: What are you, a Captain? What?

SAILOR: Not quite, sir.

RICHARD: So what do you think of the war?

SAILOR: Sir?

RICHARD: I'm sorry. Impolite. But still, what do you think of it?

SAILOR: Well, I suppose I'm—I suppose I'm sorry about it.

RICHARD: Can you think of anyone who isn't "sorry" about it?

SAILOR: I suppose not, sir.

RICHARD: Hey, I'm seeing a lot of you sailors around town lately. Why is that?

SAILOR: Fleet Week, sir.

RICHARD: Ah yes, "Fleet Week".

SAILOR: Do you mind if I use the head, sir?

RICHARD: The what? Oh, right, lingo. Straight back and to the right.

SAILOR: Thank you.

(The SAILOR *exits. Just as he does, the door flings open and in comes* PATRICIA. *She has a pair of dark glasses on and is carrying several bags from upscale shops. She speaks immediately upon entering.)*

PATRICIA: Do you see a painted target in the middle of my forehead?

RICHARD: I do not.

PATRICIA: Then why is the world trying to kill me?

RICHARD: Does someone I know have a case of the grumpy grumps?

PATRICIA: It's more than just that—it's the "tone" of things out there. It's dissonant. It's the tone of everyone I come into contact with. How we speak to one another—how we don't. How we look at one another, how we won't. Oh, and the cabbie I had today—

RICHARD: Don't tell me: he didn't get you to your nail appointment on time and he had a name with seven successive consonants in it. And so you see him and his unpronounceable name as proof positive that the world is trying to kill you.

PATRICIA: I only wanted to vent, Richard. What is the point of being married if we can't be unattractive to one another?

RICHARD: I thought the point of getting married was to make your father feel better before he died?

PATRICIA: No, you're forgetting. That was the sentimental reason we leaked to friends. The real reason was because you can't make money and you knew my family had lots of it.

(The SAILOR *enters.* PATRICIA *turns, more than a little taken aback.)*

PATRICIA: Oh—uhm, well, hello.

SAILOR: Ma'am.

*(*PATRICIA *looks back to* RICHARD.*)*

PATRICIA: Richard?

RICHARD: Darling.

PATRICIA: Why is the man from the Cracker Jack box in our living room?

RICHARD: He's not the man from the Cracker Jack box, he's a sailor. And as far as I can tell, we've adopted him.

PATRICIA: Oh! Oh, no, not tonight. Susan!

RICHARD: What about Susan?

PATRICIA: *(To* SAILOR*)* I am so sorry.

RICHARD: You were saying something about Susan?

PATRICIA: She got one of these. *(Gesturing toward* SAILOR*)* She got one of these—

RICHARD: — you mean human beings?

PATRICIA: No, sailorpeople, and she had me sign up for— *(To* SAILOR*)* I cannot believe I forgot this. I am so sorry. Will you forgive me?

SAILOR: Oh, I under—

RICHARD: —wait, Susan "got one of them?" What are you talking about?

PATRICIA: It is such an adorable thing. *(To* SAILOR*)* I am so sorry. *(Back to* RICHARD*)* You sign up. You volunteer to you know, feed them for a night and do their laundry and—And they come to you—they come to you like—

RICHARD: —like they too were living entities?

PATRICIA: No, I know, —this sounds awful, the way I'm describing it, I am so sorry. No, Susan even sewed one of their jackets for them. Their pea coat jacket things—

RICHARD: *Susan* sewed something?

PATRICIA: Not—you know, herself—she supervised it. *(To* SAILOR*)* Susan's my nearest and dearest.

(The SAILOR *politely nods.)*

RICHARD: Well, the least we could do is feed him.

PATRICIA: Of course we should.

RICHARD: We'd adopt you, but we'd be awful parents.

PATRICIA: We would be, you'd starve to death.

SAILOR: I don't mind just catching a hot dog somewhere, really.

RICHARD: A "hot dog?" Bite your tongue.

PATRICIA: We wouldn't hear of it.

RICHARD: Let's whip up some chicken.

PATRICIA: Yes, a quick *picante*.

RICHARD: I'll go to the corner.

PATRICIA: Go to Rimaldi's and get four, no, six breasts. *(To* SAILOR*)* Are you hungry?

SAILOR: I could eat a little something, ma'am.

*(*RICHARD *grabs his coat, moves to the door.)*

RICHARD: Anything else, fairy princess?

PATRICIA: More chilled Montrachet.

*(*RICHARD *opens the door, turns back.)*

RICHARD: Wait?

PATRICIA: What?

RICHARD: I'm leaving my wife alone with a sailor who's passing through town.

(The SAILOR *blushes.)*

SAILOR: Oh, you don't have to worry about—

PATRICIA: —wait, why shouldn't he worry? Am I that grotesque?

SAILOR: No, ma'am, I was just—

RICHARD: Back in a jiff!

*(*RICHARD *leaves, slams the door.* PATRICIA *and the* SAILOR *just stand there, awkward silence for a moment, then)*

PATRICIA: I had a grandfather in the navy.

SAILOR: Yes ma'am.

PATRICIA: Yes. Oh and please, enough with the "ma'am". I know it's polite, but every time you say it it's a sword through the heart of my deeply held delusion that I'm still—you know—alive.

SAILOR: Yes, ma— I mean...

PATRICIA: First trip to New York?

SAILOR: It is.

PATRICIA: What do you think?

SAILOR: It's bigger. Bigger than I thought.

PATRICIA: You don't come from a big city.

SAILOR: No.

PATRICIA: Where do you come from?

SAILOR: Oh, a little place outside Little Rock.

PATRICIA: Does it have a name?

SAILOR: Well, it's a little embarrassing.

PATRICIA: More embarrassing than say, forgetting dinner?

SAILOR: I think so.

PATRICIA: What's the name, I won't laugh.

SAILOR: Turkeyscratch.

PATRICIA: Say again?

SAILOR: Turkeyscratch.

PATRICIA: "Turkeyscratch." You come from "Turkeyscratch, Arkansas"?

SAILOR: That's right.

PATRICIA: I think Turkeyscratch is a fantastic name.

SAILOR: Why would you say that?

PATRICIA: It has a built in "jerk meter" in it. Only jerks would make fun of it.

SAILOR: Huh.

PATRICIA: Think back to all the people you've known, since the beginning of your consciousness of actually knowing where you came from. Think of all the people who laughed at the name of your town, and tell me if one of them, even one of them was not a jerk.

(The SAILOR *thinks for a good long while.)*

SAILOR: Huh, whaddya know.

PATRICIA: See. Jerk meters come in handy, trust me. Are you married?

SAILOR: I hope to be soon, ma'am.

PATRICIA: So you're engaged.

SAILOR: Not quite yet, no.

PATRICIA: In the planning stages?

SAILOR: I guess you could say that.

PATRICIA: What's her name?

SAILOR: Emily.

PATRICIA: Pretty name.

SAILOR: It sure is. I just like sayin' it. "Emily."

PATRICIA: How long have you known each other?

SAILOR: Oh, I've known Emily for—most of my life, I guess.

PATRICIA: Hometown sweetheart. That's wonderful. Do you have a picture?

SAILOR: Yes ma'am.

(He takes out a picture, shows PATRICIA.*)*

PATRICIA: Oh, she's very pretty.

SAILOR: Thank you.

PATRICIA: So what are you waiting for?

SAILOR: Well, I suppose just the right time.

PATRICIA: There is no right time, believe me.

SAILOR: Sorry?

PATRICIA: I mean you should just ask her. If it's meant to be, it's meant to be.

SAILOR: Well, I was thinking I would just—talk to her a little bit first, you know.

PATRICIA: What, prepare her, what?

SAILOR: Yeah, just to get—you know, a little acquainted with her and stuff.

PATRICIA: "Acquainted" with her? You—you do know her, don't you?

SAILOR: Oh, Emily grew up only three short blocks from me.

PATRICIA: But I mean, you've dated.

SAILOR: Oh yeah, I've dated.

PATRICIA: No, I mean—Emily.

SAILOR: Oh she dated a couple fellas from town, but, there was nothin' serious there.

PATRICIA: No, pay attention to me here. Listen to what I'm asking you. Have you, yourself, ever dated Emily?

SAILOR: No, not myself, no.

PATRICIA: Well, then—

SAILOR: —I'm just a little shy is all. I was thinking it might be better to go off and "see the world" as they say. I figured once I, you know, saw more of the world and stuff—I'd have more to talk to her about.

PATRICIA: You're telling me you've never talked to her.

SAILOR: Not in—so many words, no. But I've nodded to her. You know, toward her. In her general direction.

PATRICIA: And you have a picture of her in your wallet.

SAILOR: Oh, she was in my sister's class. I just cut it out of the yearbook. Kind of strange, huh?

PATRICIA: Not at all.

SAILOR: Do you have any children?

PATRICIA: Children? Me? No. No, no children. My artists are my children. I have a gallery downtown.

SAILOR: Well, I'm sorry for asking. I guess it wasn't too polite of me.

PATRICIA: Oh, don't even—I have issues to be sure, but not about that.

SAILOR: "Issues", ma'am?

PATRICIA: Oh, it's just an expression. I love children. I think they're indispensable, especially in regard to our need to re-populate the earth every once in awhile.

SAILOR: Yes, ma'am, no doubt.

PATRICIA: That was a joke by the way.

SAILOR: Oh yeah, yeah, I got that. Now, how did you all meet?

PATRICIA: Oh, Richard and I? It was a blind date. Well, sort of blind. He makes films.

SAILOR: Mr. Richard does?

PATRICIA: That's right.

SAILOR: Wow, a movie maker.

PATRICIA: Oh no, be careful. Richard does not make "movies." He makes films. There's a big difference.

SAILOR: What difference is that?

PATRICIA: Well, as far as I could make out, movies people want to see. Films on the other hand, people have to be talked into seeing.

SAILOR: Huh.

PATRICIA: No, Richard makes films. And they are— especially were, very provocative, very exquisite, really. He really had a very great talent. And I saw a couple of them in college and a friend of mine knew him and so I asked her to set us up. And the rest is—well, revisionist history I suppose you could call it.

SAILOR: It must be nice.

PATRICIA: What is that?

SAILOR: Geez, just all of it. Movies. Films, I mean. And college and all that.

PATRICIA: Yes, actually. Come to think of it—I suppose it was.

(RICHARD *comes through the door with a bag from the store.*)

RICHARD: I went down to Altoni's.

(PATRICIA *takes the bag, heads toward the kitchen, then turns.*)

PATRICIA: Richard, ask him where's he's from.

RICHARD: Why?

PATRICIA: I want to prove a theory.

RICHARD: Where are ya from?

SAILOR: Turkeyscratch, Arkansas.

(RICHARD *lets out a huge belly laugh.* PATRICIA *looks over at the* SAILOR.)

PATRICIA: See? Works every time. Set the table, Richard.

(PATRICIA *takes the bag into the kitchen.* RICHARD *starts to set the dining table, the* SAILOR *helps.*)

RICHARD: Did Patricia tell you what I do by any chance?

SAILOR: Yes sir, you make movies. Films, sir, sorry.

RICHARD: I had an idea for one when I was getting the chicken. And you're the inspiration for it.

SAILOR: *I* am, sir?

RICHARD: Have you ever heard of a film called *On The Town*?

SAILOR: No, sir.

RICHARD: Well there's no reason you should have. Complete piece of crap, neo-colonialist idealistic tripe totally manufactured to ease us into the post war lethargy that has led this country into every so called "conflict" since then.

SAILOR: Gee whiz, one movie did all that?

RICHARD: The point is, it was about three sailors, "on the town" as it were—and they run around New York and burst into song for no apparent reason whatsoever. Any real sailor would look at it with nothing but disdain. You've been in town a couple days, right? Have you burst into song yet?

SAILOR: Not that I remember, sir.

RICHARD: Exactly. So listen to this: My idea is to show the underbelly of all that.

SAILOR: The "underbelly"?

RICHARD: That's right, the other side of it: "Off The Town".

SAILOR: "Off The Town"?

RICHARD: That's what I would call it. "Off The Town". Whadya think?

SAILOR: Well, that sure would be interesting.

RICHARD: And I would want to use non-actors.

SAILOR: "Non-actors"?

RICHARD: That's right. We wouldn't need any celebrity pretty boys. I'm talking about real people. Maybe real sailors, even.

SAILOR: Gee whiz, really?

RICHARD: Well sure, why not?

SAILOR: And the real sailors. They wouldn't be actors.

RICHARD: They would be non actors.

SAILOR: But they would be non actors acting, right?

RICHARD: They would act, but they wouldn't be acting. That's the difference.

SAILOR: I'm not sure I—

RICHARD: —the real sailors would be non actors in a non scripted narrative about exactly what it's like to be in New York on leave, or liberty or whatever you call it.

SAILOR: I see.

RICHARD: I would just give them parameters. "This is Times Square, this is a homeless guy urinating in a bush," and we just see what happens.

SAILOR: So you would be making a movie about them?

RICHARD: A "movie?"

SAILOR: I'm sorry sir. You would just be making a— I mean they would get off the ship and without them even knowing they were actors, you would be making a film about them.

RICHARD: I think you're a little confused.

SAILOR: I am, sir.

RICHARD: I'm a filmmaker.

SAILOR: Yes, sir.

RICHARD: Do you think when someone points a camera
at you, say, on the street and they say: "Hey, sailor,
let me take a picture." And you smile for the camera.
Would you say you're acting naturally?

SAILOR: No sir.

RICHARD: You're being polite maybe, but you're not
acting naturally.

SAILOR: No, sir.

RICHARD: Well that's my point. I point a camera at three
sailors, non actors with no script and no idea what the
structure of the narrative is—until it happens.

SAILOR: Okay, sir.

(Pause, RICHARD *takes a drink, relaxes.)*

SAILOR: And what is "it," sir?

RICHARD: Let's at least agree that what is real is what
goes on in front of the camera—not behind it. Can we
at least agree on that?

SAILOR: Okay, sir.

RICHARD: What's *not* real is all the *mishegas* we go
through behind the camera to manufacture what
actually exists in front of it. Do you see the distinction?

SAILOR: Gee whiz, sir—

RICHARD: —see that's why all these film school
pinheads end up making cereal commercials the
rest of their lives. Because they have no idea. Why
is something, just because it's manufactured, not
considered real? And more to the point, why don't
colleges offer courses of study in contradiction?

SAILOR: I'm not sure, sir.

RICHARD: Of course you're not. You're not polluted yet. You haven't been to college, have you?

SAILOR: Just one or two credits, sir.

RICHARD: Well stop right there. That's enough. That's all you need. Why don't colleges have courses in contradiction? I'll tell you why. Because it would scare the living daylights out of them, that's why. Voltaire was the last brilliant light not scared of contradicting himself. Intellectual discourse in this country is dead.

SAILOR: Gee whiz, sir, you sure are smart.

RICHARD: No, I'm not. I'm a wanker dilettante idiot.

(PATRICIA *enters with salad bowls on a tray.*)

PATRICIA: What are you torturing our poor guest about?

RICHARD: I have an idea for a film.

PATRICIA: Is it about the "underbelly" of something.

RICHARD: Here we go.

SAILOR: Why yes ma'am, it is. How did you know that?

RICHARD: She's being sarcastic.

SAILOR: "Ma'am"?

PATRICIA: It's a running joke. I hope you like vinaigrette.

SAILOR: Very much, thank you.

RICHARD: It's a running joke to you. To the one slighted, it's a smear.

PATRICIA: Richard is addicted to finding the underbelly of everything. Especially happiness.

RICHARD: I wouldn't say that.

PATRICIA: What's the idea?

RICHARD: "Off The Town."

PATRICIA: Underbelly of "On the Town".

SAILOR: That's right!

RICHARD: Now don't rush to judgment on this one.

PATRICIA: That is juvenile even for you. What an awful idea. Are you kidding me? That's the kind of idea some trust fund pot head comes up with after sucking on a pipe for two weeks. Are you kidding me? Sailors, right? And let me guess, you follow them around and blah blah blah our country is one big lie and blah blah blah. What a worthless, stupid, insipid piece of crap idea. I forgot the rolls.

(PATRICIA *turns, goes into the kitchen. Awkward silence*)

SAILOR: Gee whiz, sorry, sir.

RICHARD: No, she's right, it's a stupid idea.

(PATRICIA *comes back out with rolls, puts them on the table.* RICHARD *remains seated, the* SAILOR *stands up.*)

PATRICIA: What is that?

SAILOR: Ma'am?

PATRICIA: What are you doing?

SAILOR: Oh, I'm just uh—

PATRICIA: Richard, he stood for me.

(RICHARD *suddenly stands.*)

RICHARD: Well, I was just about to.

PATRICIA *(To* SAILOR*)* Thank you very much.

SAILOR: Thank you for your hospitality.

(PATRICIA *sits, the* SAILOR *and* RICHARD *follow.*)

RICHARD: Well, can we eat? I don't know about you, but I'm famished.

PATRICIA: Richard.

RICHARD: What?

(PATRICIA *nods in the direction of the* SAILOR *who is bowing his head in prayer.*)

RICHARD: Oh, sorry.

PATRICIA: —shush!

RICHARD: Well, I'm sorry!

(RICHARD *makes a pathetic attempt to clasp his hands together, trying to emulate the "prayer position".*)

PATRICIA: What are you doing?

RICHARD: I'm trying to—

PATRICIA: Stop it!

(*The* SAILOR *lifts his head up, quickly crosses himself and turns to* PATRICIA.)

SAILOR: This salad looks awful good.

PATRICIA: Oh, please, it's nothing.

(*The* SAILOR *looks to* PATRICIA *to see if she's going to start eating.*)

PATRICIA: Go ahead and start.

SAILOR: Thank you.

(*The* SAILOR *starts to eat. Awkward silence for a little while until*)

RICHARD: So, good looking sailor like you. Girl in every port, eh?

SAILOR: Sir?

RICHARD: Well, I mean you're single aren't you? Travel all over the world. I imagine one of the perks to all that is all the chippies you meet.

PATRICIA: Are you trying your hand at male bonding, Richard? Because if you are, it's terribly awkward to watch.

RICHARD: Oh come on. Young buck out in the world. Say, does the navy set you up with whores? I mean, do they condone it or do they just look the other way?

PATRICIA: Richard—

SAILOR: —well, sir, I—I really wouldn't know about that.

RICHARD: "Wouldn't know about that?" What the heck kind of sailor are you? You don't drink and now you're telling me you don't get whores? Next thing you'll be telling me is you're a virgin. (*He laughs loudly.*) You're not a frickin' virgin are ya?

(RICHARD *laughs again. The* SAILOR *and* PATRICIA *continue to eat as* RICHARD's *laughter dies down.*)

RICHARD: Well, wait, are ya?

PATRICIA: Trust me, Richard. You don't have to worry about our new friend here. He does just fine. He showed me a picture of his girlfriend. His fiancée actually.

(*The* SAILOR *turns, looks at her.*)

RICHARD: Really?

PATRICIA: Oh yes. You see Richard, some men don't need to buy whores. Some men can attract women all by themselves.

RICHARD: Well, good for you. Good for you ya young scamp, ya!

(RICHARD *hits the* SAILOR *on the arm, winking at him.*)

SAILOR: Thank you, sir. (*Pause, then to* PATRICIA)
And thank you, ma'am.

(PATRICIA *flashes him a little smile.*)

RICHARD: Hey I don't know whether Patricia happened to mention this to you, but I have a little bit of—well, I guess you could call it "military experience" in a way.

SAILOR: Really, sir?

PATRICIA: Tell me you're not going where I think you are.

RICHARD: Well it was boot camp wasn't it?

PATRICIA: For filmmakers. Are you actually going to draw a comparison?

RICHARD: Well we "shot" things didn't we? We shot with our cameras.

PATRICIA: Do you even have the capacity to be self aware?

RICHARD: I am simply relating an experience of my own.

SAILOR: I'd like to hear about it, sir.

RICHARD: There, see.

PATRICIA: It was *film* camp!

RICHARD: I'll have you know they would roust us out of bed—sometimes at the crack of eight in the morning.

PATRICIA: The horror.

SAILOR: Well, that could be pretty early for some people.

RICHARD: You bet your behind it was early. And there were lines for food. Just like in the navy.

PATRICIA: Yes, it's good to know that if we ever come under attack again, there's an army of slightly overweight metrosexual filmmakers out there ready to protect us.

RICHARD: That's hardly fair.

PATRICIA: Providing of course the lighting is right.

RICHARD: What are you implying?

PATRICIA: Nothing, Richard. I would just like to call to your attention that once, thousands of years ago, when we all used to congregate around a campfire, everyone had a purpose. There were the hunters and the gatherers. There were the men that protected the camp. There were the women that tended to the children and made sure that they didn't roll into the fire. I don't recall reading however—about the role of the "camp intelligentsia". Those stout few who would sit around the camp's perimeter and posit about the meaning of the campfire or whether the stars above were proof of a higher power or just little balls of blue fire. No, Richard, back then, those individuals were eaten by mountain lions. And that was as it should be, don't you agree *(To* SAILOR*)* How do you like your dressing?

SAILOR: It's very good, thank you.

PATRICIA: I'm so glad.

RICHARD: So let me get this straight: I'm irrelevant because if I were a caveman, I would look at the stars and wonder about them, rather than running off and killing an antelope? Do I have that right?

PATRICIA: That isn't what I said.

RICHARD: Only because you're not honest enough to put it in those terms. But in essence, there's no place for the likes of me because I can't chase down a wild boar.

PATRICIA: No, there's a place for you. It's just not what it used to be.

RICHARD: So I am—functionally irrelevant.

PATRICIA: You could put it any way you want to Richard. We are what we are.

RICHARD: Oh, we are indeed!

SAILOR: I fell out of a plane, once.

(Both RICHARD *and* PATRICIA *look twice at the* SAILOR *as he continues to eat.)*

PATRICIA: I'm sorry, what? What did you—

SAILOR: I fell out of a plane.

RICHARD: You mean you—you mean you *jumped* out of a plane. With a parachute.

SAILOR: No sir, I didn't have a parachute on.

PATRICIA: And the plane was—the plane was in the air?

SAILOR: Yes, ma'am.

RICHARD: Well how many feet? How many feet in the air?

SAILOR: They tell me it was almost five thousand feet, sir.

(The SAILOR *continues eating.* RICHARD *and* PATRICIA *just look at him.)*

PATRICIA: Well is that all you're going to say?

SAILOR: I just thought it was an interesting fact, ma'am. I thought it would be good to bring up as a part of the dinner conversation.

PATRICIA: Well yes, I would say something like that does certainly qualify as an "interesting fact." And I'd like to hear a little more about it if you wouldn't mind.

SAILOR: Oh, it was no big deal, I was just goofin' around with a couple of my buddies in the back of a C-130 awhile back. We were on a training deal with it, learning how to stack up the pallets in back, and the pilot was taking us up for a couple test runs and a couple of my buds and I started horsing around, you know, in the storage area and Tommy Baffuto, a good buddy of mine started to really get on me. He was just

pummeling me, you know, climbing up my back,
giving me wedgies, the whole nine yards and all I
remember was him sort of pushing me real hard up
against what I thought was the wall but instead it
turned out to be the little side cargo door and "boom"
—first thing I know, all I hear is the sound of sucking
air and I remember seeing Tommy's face just looking
at me kind of strange because apparently somebody
forgot to bolt the door and out I went. Boy, that sure
was something.

(The SAILOR *goes back to eating.* PATRICIA *and* RICHARD
just look at him. A long pause, then)

PATRICIA: And...!?

SAILOR: Yes, ma'am?

RICHARD: What happened after that?

SAILOR: Well after that all of it was kind of a blur.
I just remember Tommy's face looking kind of horrified
at me. But after I fell through the clouds and started
what you might call the "free fall", all of it was kind
of beautiful and peaceful to tell you the truth.

PATRICIA: "Beautiful and peaceful"? Well, what
happened when you—I mean how did you—

SAILOR: Well Esperanzo, the doctor from our unit
explained it to me later on. He thinks I ended up not
dying because of a combination of things.

RICHARD: And they were?

SAILOR: Well, he said the fact that there was a
crosswind, the fact that some old rubber covered
telephone wires slowed me down just before I hit the
ground and the fact that I landed on a grassy hill just
at the right angle. All those things were in my favor,
he said.

RICHARD: No doubt.

SAILOR: Yes, sir. Plus he said the fact that I was relaxed going down. That I didn't tense up or try to fall on my feet. He said that's what probably saved me in the end. That and the fact that it rained the night before. I made the cross wind a kind of pillow for myself and just kind of leaned back and enjoyed the view.

RICHARD: How could you—wait, but, how could you—

SAILOR: —and the countryside was awful pretty. All the rolling hills around the base. And it was late September, so the leaves were just turning.

PATRICIA: But...but...

RICHARD: So what happened when you hit the ground?

SAILOR: Oh, I stood right up. I just got right up and started walking across the field like nothing happened at all. As it turns out I did break quite a few bones in my leg and about forty or fifty in my back and shoulders, but the doc told me that adrenaline had kicked in by then—and that made it possible for me to just walk across the field and right into the ambulance. One thing I'll never forget is how those ambulance guys just looked at me. They just stood there, staring at me while I climbed all by myself right into the back of the ambulance. They even turned the siren off. And the farmer who owned the field I fell in, he came out to look at me too. And all the time, nobody said a single word. And for days after that people just sort of stared at me, and some even came up to me and touched me on my arm or hand or whatever just for good luck. It was quite an event, it really was. It's one of those things I don't think I'll ever forget as long as I live. These tomatoes are delicious, ma'am.

PATRICIA: I'm glad you like them.

(There's a considerable pause as the SAILOR *continues to eat his salad.* PATRICIA *and* RICHARD *remain almost frozen, then:)*

PATRICIA: Perhaps Richard can cite a similar experience at film camp. Can you Richard?

RICHARD: What?

PATRICIA: At film camp. No doubt you could cite something similarly adventurous from your week at film camp. You know, the one that took place in Aspen. During the spring. At a Marriott.

RICHARD: Well, I—

SAILOR: Did you fall out of a plane, too sir?

RICHARD: No, no, of course not. But we did go on uhm—we did go on hikes. You know, rather healthy little jaunts up in the surrounding uh—you know, usually with nothing more than a single bottle of water with us.

SAILOR: Wow.

(The SAILOR *continues to eat as* RICHARD *looks across at* PATRICIA.*)*

RICHARD: Do you think that was fair?

PATRICIA: What?

RICHARD: Doing that.

PATRICIA: Doing what exactly?

(An awkward silence as PATRICIA *and* RICHARD *just stare at one another. The* SAILOR *continues to eat as* RICHARD *puts his fork down, then slowly stands up. He just stands there as the sailor looks up at him.)*

SAILOR: Is there—is there anything wrong, sir?

*(RICHARD *doesn't respond. He simply pushes his chair under the table and slowly walks to the middle of the room.*

The SAILOR *watches him curiously as* PATRICIA *continues eating.)*

PATRICIA: Don't look at him.

SAILOR: What?

PATRICIA: Don't pay any attention to him. It's exactly what he wants. Focus on your salad.

SAILOR: What?

PATRICIA: Just keep your eyes on your salad.

(The SAILOR *self consciously looks at his salad as* RICHARD *slowly collapses to his knees. The* SAILOR *looks over at him.)*

SAILOR: But he just dropped to his knees, ma'am.

PATRICIA: Did you hear me? I said don't look.

*(*RICHARD *slowly lies on his side, contorting himself into a full fetal position. The sailor can't help but look)*

SAILOR: Gee whiz ma'am. Now he's crumpled up like a baby.

*(*RICHARD *puts his thumb in his mouth and starts to rock himself back and forth on the floor)*

PATRICIA: It's a new methodology his latest moron therapist got him on. I had my therapist look into it. It's total bullcrap.

SAILOR: But he looks so sad.

PATRICIA: Of course he looks sad. He's a grown man sucking his thumb and rocking back and forth in the middle of the dining room for cripes sake.

SAILOR: Gee whiz.

PATRICIA: Don't look. If we ignore it, it won't give him the narcissistic rush he's craving. So, how old were you when you joined the navy?

SAILOR: Oh, uhm—well, I was—

(RICHARD *starts to get up)*

PATRICIA: Stay focused on me.

SAILOR: Okay. Well, I joined when I was-

PATRICIA: Was your father in the navy also?

SAILOR: No, actually, he—

(RICHARD *walks over to the table, pulls out the chair and sits
down again.)*

PATRICIA: Answer my question.

SAILOR: I'm sorry, what was the question again, ma'am?

PATRICIA: Richard, would you like anymore salad?

RICHARD: Thank you, Patricia, no. If you'll excuse me.
I'm going to go out for a little air.

SAILOR: Actually, sir, maybe I should go. We're
shipping out real early tomorrow.

RICHARD: No, you stay. I'm just feeling a little woozy.
I'll be back in a few minutes.

PATRICIA: Alright, Richard.

(RICHARD *gets up, moves to the door and exits. An awkward
silence. The* SAILOR *concentrates on his salad.)*

PATRICIA: You're very sweet to act like you're not you
know—freaked out.

SAILOR: I'm not freaked out, ma'am.

PATRICIA: And why is that?

SAILOR: Oh, I've been on a ship for six months at a time.
I've seen a lot of strange things.

PATRICIA: You've seen things as strange as what just
happened here?

SAILOR: Oh, much stranger than that. Are you always so
mean to him?

(SAILOR *goes back to eating.* PATRICIA *just looks at him.*)

PATRICIA: Sorry?

SAILOR: Mr. Richard. Are you always so mean to him?

PATRICIA: You think I'm mean to him?

SAILOR: Do you not like him very much?

PATRICIA: I think it's a little more complicated than that.

SAILOR: I'm sure you're right, ma'am.

(*Another awkward silence*)

PATRICIA: Although I am curious why you think I'm mean to him.

SAILOR: Well, just the way you talk to him. You all don't talk as much as sword fight with each other—except with words.

PATRICIA: Well, that's a pointed observation.

SAILOR: Is that right?

PATRICIA: That was an inadvertent pun by the way.

SAILOR: Sorry, ma'am?

PATRICIA: Well, you alluded to swords, and I called it a "pointed" observation.

SAILOR: Oh, that is a very funny pun, yes, ma'am.

PATRICIA: Relationships are complicated—we didn't start out like this, you know.

SAILOR: Like how?

PATRICIA: Like how we are now. Fetal positions and sword fighting.

SAILOR: No, ma'am.

PATRICIA: Part of the pain of a relationship evolving into—or maybe de-evolving into something—is being conscious of it at the same time that it's happening. Do you understand that?

SAILOR: Yes, ma'am, I do. But then that's part of the pain of living in general, isn't it?

PATRICIA: Why yes, it is. Why that, what you just said—that was rather pointed as well.

SAILOR: Yes, ma'am. I suppose once in awhile the pea does find it's way into the hole.

PATRICIA: We New Yorkers must seem a little strange to you, huh?

SAILOR: Oh, I think you all are great. A tad—what's that word? Yeah, a tad "provincial," but otherwise—I think you all are first rate.

PATRICIA: Wait, did you just call us "provincial"?

SAILOR: Why, yes, ma'am, I guess I did. I don't mean any offense at all—it's just sort of a observation, I guess.

PATRICIA: Well that's a bit of a stretch, wouldn't you say?

SAILOR: Why would that be, ma'am?

PATRICIA: Well, maybe we're not on the same wavelength when it comes to the definition of "provincial".

SAILOR: Geez, maybe we're not.

PATRICIA: When I think of someone being "provincial," I think of them as being small minded, prejudiced in their views and not being open to differing influences, especially philosophically.

SAILOR: Huh, what do ya know—that's how I think of "provincial" too.

PATRICIA: Is that right?

SAILOR: I guess it all depends on which side of the pot you're pissin' in, huh ma'am?

PATRICIA: Yes, which "side of the pot," no doubt.

(PATRICIA *goes to pour another drink,* SAILOR *turns to her.*)

SAILOR: I want you to know I appreciate your kindness as well, ma'am.

PATRICIA: About what?

SAILOR: Well the way you didn't act all freaked out about my never talking to Emily and all. I know that isn't usual. I suppose I should have just kept my mouth shut about it.

PATRICIA: Well, we all have our little peccadilloes, don't we?

SAILOR: I suppose you're right.

PATRICIA: You're a very interesting young man.

SAILOR: Well, I guess I'll take that as a compliment.

PATRICIA: I meant it as one.

(PATRICIA *refills her drink once more, turns to* SAILOR.)

PATRICIA: What was it you said about "shipping out" tomorrow? What does that mean, exactly?

SAILOR: Oh, just that I'll be moving along.

PATRICIA: Yes, but what does that mean?

SAILOR: Well, we get orders, you know. And I'll be moving onto my next orders.

PATRICIA: But where? Where are your next orders?

SAILOR: Well, I'm not—I'm not really supposed to say, ma'am.

(*Pause*)

PATRICIA: You're going to where the fighting is, aren't you?

SAILOR: I'm really not supposed to say.

PATRICIA: But you are, aren't you? You're going to where the fighting is.

(Suddenly the smoke alarm goes off in the kitchen.)

PATRICIA: Chicken!

(PATRICIA runs into the kitchen as RICHARD slowly opens the door and walks in.)

RICHARD: Is that smoke?

SAILOR: I believe so, sir.

RICHARD: Is there a fire?

SAILOR: Not that I know of.

(The smoke alarm turns off. PATRICIA emerges from the kitchen, fanning the air.)

PATRICIA: I don't want to talk about it. Don't anyone ask me about it. I want to act as though this never happened. I'm going to go out and get you something to eat. What do you want? I can get you a steak, Chinese, whatever you want.

SAILOR: I don't want you to go to any trouble, ma'am.

PATRICIA: It's not even an issue. You just need to tell me what you want.

SAILOR: To tell you the truth, ma'am. I wouldn't mind some Cocoa Puffs.

PATRICIA: I'm sorry?

SAILOR: Cocoa Puffs. It's a kind of cereal.

PATRICIA: I'm aware it's a kind of cereal. I'm talking about dinner.

SAILOR: Well, we can get that other stuff on the ship, but I haven't had Cocoa Puffs in a while.

RICHARD: Get the kid some Cocoa Puffs.

PATRICIA: But what about protein?

SAILOR: Oh, I don't care about that, ma'am.

RICHARD: Just get the kid some Cocoa Puffs.

(PATRICIA *puts on her jacket, grabs her purse, looks toward the* SAILOR)

PATRICIA: I am the worst adoptive mother ever.

RICHARD: Oh, come on.

SAILOR: That's not true, ma'am.

PATRICIA: No, it is. Susan took her sailor to Nirvana, last year. They had a twelve course Indian dinner.

SAILOR: I wouldn't have had fun there, ma'am.

PATRICIA: Well is there a "deluxe" sort of Cocoa Puff? Or some sort of special or superior Cocoa Puff that I could get you?

SAILOR: I think there's just regular Cocoa Puffs.

RICHARD: Will you just get the kid some Cocoa Puffs —he's cookoo for Cocoa Puffs.

SAILOR: *(Laughing)* Yes, sir.

PATRICIA: I'll be back in ten minutes.

(PATRICIA *leaves, slamming the door behind her.* RICHARD *and the* SAILOR *just look at one another, awkward, then)*

RICHARD: I owe you an apology.

SAILOR: What for?

RICHARD: The crumpling up on the floor, the— I put you in an awkward situation.

SAILOR: Oh, don't worry about that, sir.

RICHARD: And that ridiculous idea for a film. I want you to know that unlike most people, I know what an idiot I am.

SAILOR: I don't think you're an idiot, sir.

RICHARD: It's just that sometimes I—I don't know how much of myself to be.

SAILOR: Yes, sir.

RICHARD: Your generation never had this problem, did it?

SAILOR: Not sure which problem you're talking about, sir.

RICHARD: You know, the extent to which you're "allowed" to be a man. To show you're a man.

SAILOR: Don't recall having that particular problem, sir, no.

RICHARD: Let me ask you something.

SAILOR: Okay, sir.

RICHARD: How much of a man do you allow yourself to be?

SAILOR: Well, sir—I guess I never thought about it much.

RICHARD: What I wouldn't give to not think about it much. How do you do that?

SAILOR: Sir?

RICHARD: Not think about something much.

SAILOR: I'm afraid it comes naturally to me.

RICHARD: But yet you seem so grounded. You think less and know more. I think more and know less. What an existential farce is my life.

SAILOR: I think you're being a little hard on yourself there, sir.

RICHARD: My father was a "man's man" —I suppose you could say. He was distant, distracted, unforgiving. And of course completely and utterly adored by those of us who were on the receiving end of his—

SAILOR: What, sir?

RICHARD: Well, let's just say he wasn't a teddy bear and leave it at that, shall we?

SAILOR: I'm sorry.

RICHARD: What about your parents? Are they still with us?

SAILOR: Oh, yes, sir—they've been married going on thirty years now. They met in kindergarten.

RICHARD: Of course they did. You're very fortunate. Do you know that?

SAILOR: Oh, I know that, sir.

RICHARD: Do you really?

SAILOR: Sir?

RICHARD: I mean you'll forgive me—I hope, but I do have reason to wonder.

SAILOR: Wonder what, sir?

RICHARD: Well, in the final analysis, what do we know about you? You don't drink, you don't buy whores, you stand up for my wife at the dinner table, you pray, you fall out of airplanes *without* dying—and yet you claim—and I do believe you mean it, I really do— you claim to somehow understand how lucky you are. My only question is "how?" How could you truly understand how lucky you are when you don't have anything to compare it to?

SAILOR: Well, I only know what I know, sir.

RICHARD: And you're right, of course. And this is not a critique of you, it isn't—but it's easy for someone like you, isn't it?

SAILOR: Sir?

RICHARD: Well, I mean the world is—in many ways, constructed around someone like you. You're the poster boy for poster boys—and this "Sir", "Gee whiz", stuff, I mean, some of it—let's be honest, I'm sure it comes from a real place I'm sure, but some of it has to be an affectation, doesn't it? So who are you? I mean is this "you" really you? Because if it is, who *wouldn't* suffer by comparison? You're very sweet, you are— and I like you. And I know what I must seem like next to you, but don't tell me you understand when—if this you—is you—there is just no way you could. *(Pause)* I'm sorry, it's not right of me to—

SAILOR: —no, sir, you're right.

RICHARD: What?

SAILOR: You're right.

RICHARD: Could you be clearer about what it is I'm right about exactly, because I'm afraid even I'm not that sure.

SAILOR: Just that in a lot of ways, I have been lucky sir. And I'm sure sometimes I do act dumber than I am. But I don't mean any disrespect by it I really don't.

RICHARD: Of course you don't. Look, we all do it— we all "don a mask".

SAILOR: Is that right, sir?

RICHARD: Of course it is. Just like I was saying before. It's what we do behind the camera that is truly the performance. I play roles all the time.

SAILOR: Do you, sir?

RICHARD: Of course. Look, I play so many roles I sometimes forget during any given day, what role it was I began playing in the morning—so that by the time lunch comes around, I've already inhabited so many disparate characters in my "arsenal of selves," that I've been known to invite *myself* to lunch—thinking I was someone else entirely.

SAILOR: Gee whiz.

RICHARD: And as a result—I have found myself sitting alone at a restaurant expecting someone other than my genuine self to come and join me—when in point of fact, no one ever does. Because—

SAILOR: —because you were the one who invited yourself to lunch in the first place.

RICHARD: Exactly.

SAILOR: Gee whiz, sir, I feel like my head is gonna explode just thinkin' about that.

(The SAILOR *tries to keep from Laughing.)*

RICHARD: What?

SAILOR: I'm sorry, sir.

RICHARD: No, don't apologize. No, please, enjoy. Of course you should laugh. Enjoy yourself. It is funny. We need the clown. I can be the clown. I don't mind being the clown. Go ahead, laugh. Really, enjoy.

(The SAILOR *finally quells his laughter.)*

SAILOR: I'm sorry, sir. I wasn't laughing *at* you, I was—well, what's the point sir, of course I was laughin' at ya.

(They both laugh some more.)

RICHARD: I appreciate the honesty.

(They both laugh a little, together. RICHARD *raises his glass.)*

RICHARD: To honesty.

(The SAILOR *raises his)*

SAILOR: Honesty. Yes, sir.

(They both drink.)

SAILOR: Say, sir—what are your films about?

RICHARD: Well, I suppose if there were one overriding theme, it would be—that there is no overriding theme.

SAILOR: Huh. Well do you make films, all day, or—?

RICHARD: Well no, of course not, not *all* day.

SAILOR: Well, what do you during the rest of the day when you're not making films?

RICHARD: Well, I uhm—there's a lot that goes into putting a project together. There's the establishment of the uhm—of course I don't happen to be a slave to narrative, whereas a lot of directors I know might start from the basis of pure story. But for me, I usually find myself inspired by more of a tangential—uhm—and then, you know, of course there's the practical aspects of assembling a crew. And the writing. If there is any. That is, assuming it's not an improvisatory piece. But it is a process, yeah, there's a whole uh—

SAILOR: And do you—do you do that "process" here, sir?

RICHARD: You mean here physically, as in this apartment?

SAILOR: Yes, sir.

RICHARD: Well, I have an office in back, you know, but—hey, you just—you just did it, didn't you?

SAILOR: Did what, sir?

RICHARD: The thing where you—what we were just talking about, where you *seem* to not know what you're—but—but—

SAILOR: I'm not sure what you mean, sir.

RICHARD: There! Right there, you just did it again.

SAILOR: I really don't know what you mean, sir.

RICHARD: And AGAIN!

SAILOR: No, sir, really, I—

RICHARD: Stop denying it. You're brilliant. If you're brilliant, say you're brilliant! The way you brought me to this place, the way you got me here—it's like a dentist, distracting a child before he— Masterful.

SAILOR: I didn't mean to —

RICHARD: Because of course you're right.

SAILOR: About what, sir?

RICHARD: About what it is you're not saying.

SAILOR: What is it I'm not saying, sir?

RICHARD: You're just too polite and cunning—to come out and say it.

SAILOR: I'm not sure I meant to not say anything, sir.

RICHARD: No, of course you didn't. You didn't have to. You're too smart for that. But you shouldn't hold back now.

SAILOR: Hold back what, sir?

RICHARD: What you're saying to me. What you're saying to me by not saying anything. It's as clear to me as the nose on your face. I am a FRIGGING SHAM! My whole life IS A LIE! I'm a worthless PIECE OF CRAP!

SAILOR: Geez, sir, I didn't mean to not say all that.

RICHARD: Of course you did. But I mean it when I say I thank you for it.

SAILOR: No reason to thank me, sir.

RICHARD: Of course there is. My wife, who has been supporting me our entire married life, has nothing but contempt for me. And why shouldn't she? I lie on the floor and suck my thumb when I'm sad. I don't have a job. I don't make any money.

SAILOR: Gee, sir, maybe you're being a little hard on yourself.

RICHARD: Oh come on it's been the elephant in the room for years.

SAILOR: What elephant, sir?

(PATRICIA *enters with a bag.*)

RICHARD: Patricia!

PATRICIA: Yes, Richard?

RICHARD: I'm getting a job.

PATRICIA: What?

RICHARD: You heard me. I'm getting a job. A *real* job.

PATRICIA: Why?

RICHARD: Because I'M A MAN, that's why.

PATRICIA: Richard, sit down.

RICHARD: Okay. (*He sits.*)

PATRICIA: (*To* SAILOR) I found the Cocoa Puffs. And for us, Richard, I got a couple Paninis. And *you* sailor boy were wrong. There are some Cocoa Puffs that are better than others. I found the Cocoa Puffs with the "new improved taste".

SAILOR: Gee, that's great ma'am, thanks.

PATRICIA: Richard, get him some milk.

RICHARD: Yes, dear. *(He gets up, then turns back)* But I want it noted that I'm not getting the milk because you told me to. I'm doing it because it's the right thing to do.

PATRICIA: That is duly noted, Richard. Now, get the milk.

RICHARD: Alright.

(RICHARD goes into the kitchen. PATRICIA places the other food on the table, looking toward the SAILOR.)

PATRICIA: I hope he hasn't been driving you crazy.

SAILOR: Not at all, ma'am.

PATRICIA: Did you mention to him that you're "shipping out" tomorrow?

(RICHARD enters with milk.)

RICHARD: We only have whole I'm afraid.

SAILOR: That works for me, sir.

(RICHARD puts the milk down on the table, then turns to SAILOR)

RICHARD: Hey, I was thinking—stay over tonight.

SAILOR: Sir?

PATRICIA: Yes.

RICHARD: We have an extra room—and I could take you on a real tour of the city tomorrow. You could see something other than the tourist traps. What do you say?

SAILOR: I wish I could, sir.

RICHARD: Have you been to the Whitney yet?

SAILOR: The "Whitney", sir?

PATRICIA: Richard—

RICHARD: Or I could take you to a Yankee game. Have you been up there, yet?

SAILOR: Not yet, sir.

(RICHARD *starts toward bedroom.*)

RICHARD: I have a brand new pair of P Js you could use—haven't even opened the package yet.

SAILOR: Sir, I can't stay, sir, I'm sorry.

RICHARD: What? Why? It's too late to go back to the ship. We can drop you off tomorrow, after our tour.

SAILOR: Well, fact is we're shipping out real early in the morning, sir. I'm really gonna have to be moving along.

RICHARD: Oh. Oh, well—that's disappointing.

SAILOR: Yes, sir.

PATRICIA: And so you spent your last night of freedom with us. (*To* RICHARD) What an awful quirk of fate for him, wouldn't you say, Richard?

RICHARD: Well, wait a minute, you mean—you mean you're really "shipping out" tomorrow?

SAILOR: Yes, sir.

RICHARD: To where exactly?

SAILOR: I can't really say, sir.

RICHARD: "Can't really say"?

PATRICIA: Which from what I can guess, is military-speak for: "a place I might be killed".

RICHARD: Well, wait a minute. This is very upsetting.

SAILOR: Oh, you don't have to worry about me, sir.

RICHARD: Well, couldn't we just write you some kind of note, maybe to your "commanding officer person" or "ranking authority general supervisor"? Someone like that?

PATRICIA: Richard, he's not in second grade. We can't just write him a note.

SAILOR: And last I checked sir, there's no generals in the navy.

RICHARD: Well of course, I'm only trying to—

PATRICIA: —though there must be an aspect of this that *is* negotiable.

SAILOR: Ma'am?

PATRICIA: Case in point: What if we said Richard here needed an assistant?

RICHARD: But I don't need an assistant.

PATRICIA: I know that Richard. I'm only curious what would happen if we "floated" the idea.

SAILOR: Not sure that would make much of a difference, ma'am.

PATRICIA: But why wouldn't it? Are you telling me that even if we offered you a job that paid two or even three times more than the Navy does, *that* wouldn't release you from any contractual agreement you have with them?

SAILOR: I don't think it quite works that way.

RICHARD: Wait a minute, this is very upsetting. I don't like this "shipping out". I don't like the reality of it. I have a real gut feeling of sadness in my stomach about this. I'm not feeling in a safe and secure space about this right now.

(RICHARD *starts to drift toward the center of the room, like before.*)

PATRICIA: Richard so help me—if I see your thumb go anywhere near your mouth right now I'm going to break it off—right in front of you. Now you just hold it together.

SAILOR: Oh, you don't have to worry about me, sir.
I'll be back before ya know it, and then we'll be able
to go on that tour. Because I really would like to see all
those places you were talking about. The "Whitney"
—all that stuff. That all sounds fun to me.

(Pause, awkward silence)

SAILOR: But boy, right now I sure would like to dig into
those Cocoa Puffs if that's okay?

PATRICIA: What?

SAILOR: The Cocoa Puffs?

PATRICIA: Oh, right—of course. I'm so sorry. Richard.

*(The SAILOR sits at the table as PATRICIA brings over the
Cocoa Puffs and pours them in a bowl for him. Meanwhile,
RICHARD adds the milk.)*

SAILOR: Boy, I sure am glad the chicken got burned.
No offense, ma'am.

PATRICIA: No, it's fine. Dig in.

SAILOR: Thank you, ma'am.

*(The SAILOR starts to eat, obviously hungry after all this
time. PATRICIA and RICHARD stand over him, just watching
him. He looks up at them, a little awkward.)*

SAILOR: Boy, this sure is better than—what's the name
of that fancy restaurant, ma'am?

PATRICIA: Nirvana.

SAILOR: Yup, this sure is better than that I bet.

(RICHARD turns and slowly starts pacing.)

PATRICIA: What are you doing?

(RICHARD turns, faces her.)

RICHARD: There's a confluence here Patricia. Do you
feel it?

PATRICIA: Oh, please don't.

SAILOR: "A conflu" what, sir?

RICHARD: A confluence. We're standing in the middle
of what might be called an intersection of energy.
Events have conspired to come together in a way
that do nothing but compel us to act in accordance
with their demands.

PATRICIA: Oh, Richard, please—

RICHARD: Mock if you will, but you can't deny what is
obvious here. In walks this stranger into our midst. He
has come unawares. The night, the very night before his
impending journey into what? Before he goes where?
Do you realize millions have gone before you? It's as
old as time itself and a self fulfilling prophecy. And
why? To do what? To kill whom? To save what? Hear
the sound of clanging? What is that? It's the sound of
metal on metal, man, that's what. It's the ball bearings
and pistons. Because what are we, but ghosts in the
machine? And how are we less culpable? "Adopt a
Sailor?" What is that? I'll tell you what it is. It's the
period on the end of a sentence written into ancient
templates eons and eons ago so that we could keep
the chain of unbroken complicity well oiled and pliable,
that's what. "Cocoa Puffs or chicken," what difference
does it make? Trace it back.

PATRICIA: You're blathering.

RICHARD: Well come on, it's obvious: fresh faced kid
sits in the middle of a room eating Cocoa Puffs. Seems
benign enough, unless you do a little detective work.

PATRICIA: Have we come to the "underbelly" part yet?

RICHARD: —sent here, however innocently it might
seem, to have himself one more little taste of the life
he's been indoctrinated into believing he has to fight
and die for. Have some apple pie, kid. Have some ice

cream too. Trace it back. Born to live, work, fight, consume, die, live, work, fight, consume, die and for what? What are you gonna die for Turkeyscratch? Huh? What are you gonna die for?

PATRICIA: Shut up, Richard.

SAILOR: No ma'am, it's alright.

RICHARD: Don't mind Patricia and I. This is how people talk when they don't love each other any more.

SAILOR: Sir?

PATRICIA: Richard is being sardonic when what he meant to be was sincere.

RICHARD: Well come on, I don't mean anything I say with any personal disrespect, I really don't. I just want a clear answer, that's all. What are you going to die for Turkeyscratch?

PATRICIA: *(To* SAILOR*)* Don't answer him.

SAILOR: I don't mind.

RICHARD: You do realize that nothing I'm saying is personal.

SAILOR: Yes, sir, of course sir.

RICHARD: It isn't you that I'm at odds with.

PATRICIA: No of course not. Only with everything he represents and that possibly gives his life meaning.

RICHARD: Well in so many words, yes.

PATRICIA: Though, perhaps he's finding that distinction as hard to fathom as I am.

RICHARD: You'll have to forgive my wife. She's convinced there's no connection between an action and a response. That everything going to hell in a hand basket in the world now is totally unrelated to choices made years and years ago by flinty men in flinty blue suits and red ties. You see this is where we diverge somewhat, philosophically.

PATRICIA: "Diverge." How pleasantly innocuous.

RICHARD: *(To* SAILOR*)* My point is: You don't have to go.

PATRICIA: Who are you to talk to him like that?

RICHARD: A concerned citizen, that's who. And someone who cares about him.

PATRICIA: Oh, bullshit. This isn't about him. It's about you. This isn't about him and who he is—it's about you and who you're not.

RICHARD: Who *I'm* not?

PATRICIA: That's right.

RICHARD: You're embarrassing yourself, and you're drunk.

PATRICIA: Of course I'm drunk. How else could I get through another minute listening to your solipsistic drivel?

RICHARD: You need to put the glass down and get a hold of yourself, Patricia.

PATRICIA: And you need to grow a spine, half man.

RICHARD: Oh, I see. So now name calling is—

PATRICIA: —no Richard, this—THIS is how people talk when they don't love each other anymore!

(Awful awkwardness as everyone remains silent. Then, slowly, the SAILOR *gets up from the table.)*

SAILOR: Well, I—I should just—I should just let you all—I shouldn't have barged in on you like this. It wasn't very fair to you all. *(He moves closer to his bag, then turns.)* 'Cause you two are—you two are too smart for me. Watching you all talk is like being at a tennis match, my head going all—I mean I could hardly keep up with ya.

RICHARD: You don't have to go.

SAILOR: No sir, I do, I gotta—oh, and hey, you don't have to worry about me dying or nothin'. I'm too awful chicken to die. I hear the sound of a pop gun and I'm just— No, I'm no G I Joe, I could promise you that— So you don't have to worry about— *(Starts to pick up his bag, stops)* —and it is funny, sir—I mean when you really think about it. I mean, you know, you asking me about why I would go off and—I mean I wish I had some big complicated answer for ya, but to tell ya the truth there just isn't any. I mean I see all those smart people on the Sunday talk shows all talking about the "political" this and that and I hear those movie stars too, you know, talking about why it is they think my buddies and I joined up—and they'll say stuff like they didn't think we had much choice in the matter or that we do it for the money or somethin' like that and I don't mean no disrespect toward them, I don't, but I mean that just makes me laugh. I mean that just makes me chuckle, it does, and I think movie stars are great, but most of the guys I know still can't afford a place of their own—which is why so many of us live on the ship full time anyway. And besides, if we wanted to make the "big" money we'd just go work at Burger King where usually people aren't shootin' at ya. I mean usually, anyway. But I really thought that maybe I could do something, you know, maybe even just help people or something, but—well, hey, I better just— *(He starts to leave.)*

PATRICIA: Wait.

(PATRICIA runs into the kitchen. RICHARD then moves to a desk, pulls out a small box, plucking piles of large bills from it. He turns to the SAILOR again.)

RICHARD: Take this.

SAILOR: What for, sir?

RICHARD: Well, just to— for Cripes sake, for anything, treat yourself. You can't tell me they pay you enough in that damn army of yours.

SAILOR: I'm in the navy, sir.

RICHARD: You know what I mean, take it.

SAILOR: I can't take money, sir.

RICHARD: Well then just give it to a charity or something. Isn't there some kind of navy charity or something?

SAILOR: Well, I guess I can give it to the Navy Relief Society.

RICHARD: Good, then give it to them. But for cripes sake, just take it, will you? Please.

(The SAILOR *takes the money, puts it in his pocket)*

SAILOR: Yes, sir. They'll get every dollar. It sure is awful generous of you.

RICHARD: Not really.

*(*PATRICIA *re-enters with a brown bag.)*

PATRICIA: I wanted you to have something for the road.

SAILOR: Thank you, ma'am.

PATRICIA: All I had was some brie—and some soda crackers. So try to refrigerate it as soon as you can. Do they have a refrigerator on your ship?

SAILOR: Oh, yes, ma'am.

PATRICIA: Good, and there's some Ande's mints and a couple fresh kiwis as well. My God, will you listen to me? I am the worst adoptive mother ever.

SAILOR: I think you're a great adoptive mother, ma'am.

RICHARD: Something tells me you'll be the only sailor going back to the ship tonight with brie, kiwi and soda crackers.

SAILOR: I think you're probably right about that, sir.

(PATRICIA *suddenly notices something*)

PATRICIA: Oh, wait! (*She runs over to the table, grabs the box of Cocoa Puffs and stuffs it into his duffle bag*)

SAILOR: Geez, thank you, ma'am. I appreciate that. Well, I better-

(*He turns toward the door.* PATRICIA *calls out:*)

PATRICIA: Wait!

(*She runs and hugs him, hard*)

PATRICIA: You stay a chicken, you hear me? Please promise me you'll stay a chicken.

SAILOR: I promise, ma'am.

(*They let go of one another.*)

RICHARD: And for Cripes sake, don't fall out of anymore planes.

SAILOR: I won't, sir. (*He starts out.*)

PATRICIA: Oh, and Emily.

SAILOR: Ma'am?

PATRICIA: She has no idea—how lucky she is.

SAILOR: I appreciate that, ma'am. I mean—Patricia.

(*The* SAILOR *swings the bag over his shoulder, opens the door and turns back to both of them. He beams a smile toward them once more, then closes the door with a loud thud.* PATRICIA *and* RICHARD *stand perfectly still.* PATRICIA *then slowly moves toward the door, touching it as* RICHARD *moves back toward the table. He sits, listlessly picking at his food.* PATRICIA *walks over to the table as well, moving in the*

direction of one of the chairs. Then, just as she's about to sit,
RICHARD *stands for her.* PATRICIA *reacts, more than a little*
surprised. RICHARD *then walks over to her. She sits, and he*
helps push her chair in. RICHARD *then goes back to his chair*
and sits. They both look at one another as over we hear the
Prelude to Bach's Cello Suite Number One as they continue
to look at one another, a smile beginning to form on
PATRICIA's *lips as the lights fade slowly to black.)*

END OF PLAY

APPENDIX

10 minute version

This ten minute version was originally produced 9-11 September 2002 at Town Hall in New York City as part of the Brave New World event to commemorate the first anniversary of the terrorist attacks.

Setting: PATRICIA *and* RICHARD's *finely appointed dining room in their Tribeca co-op.*

Time: May, 2002

(At rise we see RICHARD *seated at the table and the young* SAILOR, *hovering near it uncomfortably. The table setting tells us dinner is over. The sailor is dressed in his dress whites, his green duffle bag leaning against a table behind him.* PATRICIA *enters with an open bottle on wine in one hand and a full glass in the other.)*

PATRICIA: *(To* SAILOR*)* All we have left is a Montrachet '97, is that okay?

SAILOR: Oh, that's fine with me, ma'am.

RICHARD: Darling, I hardly think he's that picky. *(To* SAILOR*)* No offense to you of course. Not implying at all that you're not a connoisseur—it's just that I imagine you don't much obsess about vintage.

SAILOR: No, sir, not usually.

*(*PATRICIA *pours some in the* SAILOR'*s glass. The* SAILOR *sits.)*

SAILOR: Thank you, ma'am.

PATRICIA: Oh, please, anything but "ma'am".

SAILOR: Sorry, ma'am. I mean...

PATRICIA: ...Patricia.

SAILOR: "Patricia", right.

RICHARD: Is that something they drill into you early on?

SAILOR: Sir?

RICHARD: The by rote response, the "ma'am, sir" retort. I imagine after awhile it becomes reflexive.

SAILOR: Well, I'm not sure about that, sir. I just mean it as a sign of respect.

RICHARD: Of course.

SAILOR: I guess it's something I just got used to.

PATRICIA: *(To* RICHARD*)* You're making him self conscious.

RICHARD: And you're projecting.

PATRICIA: Why is it every observation I make that you feel uncomfortable with is a "projection", while every observation you make is an "insight"? Can you rectify that cavernous disparity for me?

RICHARD: I could, but now would not be the appropriate time or place.

SAILOR: *(Re: wine)* Boy, this is good wine!

PATRICIA: I'm so glad you like it.

(PATRICIA *goes to sit. The* SAILOR *stands up.* PATRICIA *takes note.)*

PATRICIA: Oh my goodness.

SAILOR: Ma'am?

PATRICIA: Richard, he stood for me. *(She sits.)*

RICHARD: So he did.

(The SAILOR *sits)*

PATRICIA: Richard hasn't stood for me in years.

RICHARD: *(To* SAILOR*)* Just ignore our little "spats". This is how people talk when they don't love each other anymore.

SAILOR: Sir?

RICHARD: I was...kidding. I was being sardonic.

SAILOR: Oh.

PATRICIA: "Sardonic" is what people become when they don't have the balls to be truthful anymore.

SAILOR: Boy, listening to you two is—it's like a tennis match, it really is. My neck is hurtin' just listening to you. Bouncing, bouncing, back and forth. I hope you'll forgive me. I'm just having a little trouble keeping up. You both are very smart people.

PATRICIA: Now you're being sardonic.

SAILOR: No, ma'am.

RICHARD: So what is the name of this week again?

SAILOR: "Fleet Week", sir.

RICHARD: Right, "Fleet Week."

PATRICIA: I just love it. All of you running around in your crisp white uniforms. Craning up your necks.

RICHARD: You should like the uniforms. You pay for them.

PATRICIA: Oh, just ignore Richard. Richard is a humbug. Richard doesn't like the military very much. (*She pours herself another drink.*)

RICHARD: In defense of myself, that's not exactly true. It's the ethic. It's the military ethic I find myself somewhat at odds with.

PATRICIA: Oh, I think it's worse than that. I would say you were virulently anti-military. I think if the military were a race, you would be a racist.

RICHARD: I think you're exaggerating just a tad, darling. (*To* SAILOR) Please, feel perfectly welcome. When Patricia told me she was "bringing home a sailor" —you could imagine it threw me for a little loop.

SAILOR: Yes, sir.

PATRICIA: It's a program, Richard. How many times do I have to tell you that? "Adopt a Sailor." It's a program and that's what it's called.

RICHARD: Well, regardless, it's not every day your wife brings home a sailor. Or is it everyday, darling? Maybe this is just the first time you've told me about it.

PATRICIA: I don't think I'll respond to that.

SAILOR: *(Starting to stand)* Maybe this isn't the best time...

PATRICIA: *(Almost pushing him back down)* ...of course it is. Sit. *(To* RICHARD*)* Susan adopted a sailor as well. She got hers yesterday.

RICHARD: Did she?

PATRICIA: That's where I heard about it. *(To* SAILOR*)* Susan is my nearest and dearest. She was the one who showed me the flier with all the information about it. I just think it's the most adorable idea. And why shouldn't someone "adopt" you all while you're here protecting us. A hot meal, fresh laundry. We're just giving back. Someone to look after you while you're far away from hearth and home. Susan said that you were all going fast and that if I wanted to reserve one of you, I better act fast. And I did.

RICHARD: You're making him sound like a White sale at Saks.

PATRICIA: Well, it's adorable. It's an adorable little program and I'm glad to do it.

RICHARD: *(To* SAILOR*)* "Adorable"...if you haven't yet noticed, being the definitive expression.

PATRICIA: Susan is even sewing for the sailor she got. She's sewing a patch on his little sea coat. Or jacket. Or pea jacket coat...whatever you call it.

RICHARD: *Susan* is sewing?

PATRICIA: Well, she's having someone else do it...
but she *arranged* it.

RICHARD: *(To* SAILOR*)* Warms the cockles, doesn't it?

SAILOR: Well, I certainly appreciate this, ma'am.
Whoops, sorry... I mean, Patricia. The food...and all
the nice table settings and stuff.

PATRICIA: Don't be silly. It's the least we can do...
after all you do for us.

RICHARD: *(To* SAILOR*)* Ever since the attacks, my wife
has been living her life as though she were in a movie
scored by Aaron Copland.

SAILOR: Sir?

RICHARD: Actually, I've had a little military experience
myself. Well, I suppose "military like" would be closer
to the truth.

PATRICIA: Please tell me you're not going where I think
you are.

RICHARD: Well, why shouldn't I? It was "boot camp",
wasn't it?

PATRICIA: "Writers' Boot Camp."

RICHARD: Well, still, we got up early. And it was quite
regimented, it was.

SAILOR: Yes, sir.

RICHARD: I felt like...I don't know, but I felt like I was
really in the military. We would have to write drafts,
you know, of whatever we were working on. It so
happens at that time I was working on a paper
comparing and contrasting post modern neo-colonialist
novelists with the writings of eighteenth century
Calvinist clergy—which as I'm sure you could imagine,
was not exactly an easy subject to tackle. Especially at

the crack of nine—which is when they used to roust us out of our beds in the morning.

SAILOR: Yes, sir, sounds pretty complicated to me.

PATRICIA: This is really terribly embarrassing.

SAILOR: Hey, were you both here?

PATRICIA: For what?

SAILOR: When the planes came in. Where you here?

RICHARD: You mean for the tragedy?

SAILOR: Sir?

PATRICIA: Oh, don't mind Richard. He's just deflecting. He and I don't quite see "eye to eye" on this. If we did, he wouldn't use the oh so banal and neutral term "tragedy" to describe the attacks. If the word "tragedy" were a country, it would be Switzerland.

RICHARD: Are you saying it wasn't a tragedy?

PATRICIA: The sinking of the Titanic was a tragedy. What happened last September was a calculated heinous crime. An atrocity. An act of war. An attack. Hear that, city? "Attack"! *(To* SAILOR*)* If you live in the boroughs, you could call it an attack. If you live down here or on the Upper West Side and call it an "attack" —you're a fascist warmonger. "Attack" is way too accusatory. It implies fault on the part of the attacker or whoops—should I say "inciter" of said "incident." It was an "occurrence" and nothing more. That's the party line anyway.

RICHARD: *(To* SAILOR*)* You'll have to forgive her. My wife is intent on ignoring what anyone with even an elementary grasp of geopolitical confluences might call "underlying causes." To her, this came out of the blue. To those of us with a little more... "breadth of scope" ...it's simply icing on a cake left unattended in an oven years and years ago.

PATRICIA: *(To* SAILOR*)* It's my husband you should
forgive. Somehow Richard believes that if we have a
foreign policy that is seen to favor Israel, rich sexually
repressed Saudi frat boys should have the right to
incinerate fellow Muslims working as bus boys at
Windows on the World for six dollars an hour.

RICHARD: Quaint.

PATRICIA: *(To* SAILOR*)* Following his logic, a women
who gets raped is "asking for it" because she happens
to be wearing fishnet stockings. I find that a strange and
even contradictory viewpoint for a so called dyed in the
wool liberal to have, don't you?

RICHARD: Disingenuous to the core.

PATRICIA: The problem of course, is that he didn't see
it happen. Not live anyway. Not with his own eyes...
as it was happening. That's what changed my thinking.
That's the difference between me and Richard. It
always will be.

RICHARD: Here it comes.

PATRICIA: Well, it's true. *(To* SAILOR*)* I was supposed to
open the gallery early that day, but I was running late.
I was out on the terrace watering the plants when
I heard it...the engine. The engine of the first plane.
He was flying it straight down the Hudson. They say
he was following the river to navigate his way down to
the towers. Of course when I saw him fly over I knew
something was awfully wrong right away. The shadow
of a wing actually passed over me, over my little
tulips on the terrace. Planes just don't fly that close to
buildings here. Not over New York anyway. Maybe
Hong Kong, but not in New York. "Something is out
of whack," I thought, because his wings were dipping
a little. And the sound of the engine, something was
strange about it. It didn't sound right. Someone told me
later it was because "what's his name...the little creep

flying the first one...what was his name? "Atta"? He
didn't really know how to fly it. It was in the wrong
gear, or whatever you call it on planes. And there I saw
it, right in front of me. Him dipping the wing down and
almost puttering...almost puttering the plane into the
building and I remember thinking how strange it was
that I was seeing it happen, but not hearing it. But you
know, it takes a little while for the sound wave or the
shock wave or whatever you call it and I just stood
there. I don't even think I screamed. "It must be a
dream", I thought. What I just saw must be a dream.
Or maybe it was television. "This must be television I'm
watching," I thought, because it was too real to be real.
And I remember picking up my cell phone and calling
9-1-1...can you imagine how ridiculous? As though I
would be the first caller. As though no one else would
think to call. "A plane just flew into the..." I even forget
what it was I said to the operator. "A plane just..." And
then I called Richard, but he was in a class.

RICHARD: A department meeting actually.

PATRICIA: Right, a department meeting. And so I just
stood there. With my hand over my mouth. And then
the second one. That was different. Straight in. That
mother f'er knew what he was doing, oh yeah. I always
think now...how elated he must have been...the bastard
flying that one...how elated he must have been to see
the other tower on fire. It must have been like a big
green light to him. A big "how do ya do." A big happy
handshake. Him I imagine smiling when he rammed it
in. Not Atta, but the second one. I'll bet you anything
he was smiling. *(Pause. She refills her glass.)*

RICHARD: It was an awful, awful day.

PATRICIA: I cried. I cried for days straight.

SAILOR: *(To* PATRICIA, *earnest)* I'm very sorry.

PATRICIA: Thank you. *(Pause)* Richard on the other hand...

RICHARD: —Patricia—

PATRICIA: Richard and his comrades up at Columbia had a little bit of a different response.

RICHARD: You're starting to embarrass yourself.

PATRICIA: They had "forums". "Panels." Oh, it was hilarious. You should have seen them all. All these baby boomer half men with their middle age paunches and co-ed girlfriends hanging on their every word. And their Vietnam deferments still rankling their puny psyches. "Forums and panels", every other ridiculous pointless day. Why we deserved it. Why we deserved to have planes flown into our buildings.

RICHARD: *(To* SAILOR*)* See, this is what I mean by her inability to—

PATRICIA: ...no, see this...THIS, Richard, is how people talk when they don't love each other anymore.

(A long silence. The SAILOR *slowly takes the napkin off his lap and starts to get up.)*

SAILOR: Well, I better, uhm—I better get—

(The SAILOR *moves toward his duffle bag, slings it over his shoulder. He turns back to* RICHARD *and* PATRICIA.*)*

SAILOR: Well, I—I really do appreciate...you both are way too smart for me. I must have just sat there boring you. I'm sorry about that. I'm just a...sometimes down in the galley, you know, they'll have on the talk shows, you know, the news ones on Sunday mornings and all that and I'll just look up at 'em and I'll marvel at the— not that I don't understand 'em, I do. I mean I had a year or so of college. Not a big college like Columbia, but—but I think it's great the talks you must have up there. I think it's good to talk about it. I do, really.

Maybe by your talking about it—maybe stuff like what happened won't happen again. I admire you for it, I really do.

(RICHARD *just looks at him.*)

SAILOR: As for me, I wish I could see things that complicated but I was out in the middle of the Indian Ocean when it happened. I remember we saw it on television and then that night I had duty on deck again, as usual, and I remember looking up at the sky and sure enough, seeing every star out that night that I saw the night before. Stupid, I know, but—that's what I was thinking. What with all that just happened that day, all the awfulness and the meanness and the evil that they tried to do to us—every star I saw the night before was still right up there. And I thought, well, "that's good". That's a good thing. And it was beautiful that night. Just a beautiful, beautiful star filled night.

(RICHARD *and* PATRICIA *remain perfectly still.*)

SAILOR: Anyway, I...I sure do appreciate your— you have a good night, now.

(*The* SAILOR *turns, goes to the door, opens it. He turns back, smiling sweetly toward them, then closes the door.* PATRICIA *gets up, takes a few steps toward the door then stops. She looks back at* RICHARD. RICHARD *looks at her as the lights fade slowly to black.*)

END OF PLAY